Project Scien

Materials
and their Properties

Margaret Abraitis, Angela Deighan,
Brian Gallagher, Brian Smith and Michael Toner

Brilliant Publications

We hope you and your class enjoy using this book. The other books in the Project Science series are:

Life Processes and Living Things   ISBN 1 897675 70 4
Physical Processes   ISBN 1 897675 69 0

If you would like to order these books or find out about others published by Brilliant Publications, please write to the address given below.

Published by Brilliant Publications, The Old School Yard, Leighton Road, Northall, Dunstable, Bedfordshire LU6 2HA, UK
www.brilliantpublications.co.uk

Written by Margaret Abraitis, Angela Deighan, Brian Gallagher, Brian Smith and Michael Toner
Illustrated by Pat Murray
Cover photograph by Martyn Chillmaid

Printed by the Book Factory in London, UK

Contents

Introduction

Welcome to what we hope is a comprehensive attempt to address the requirements of the National Curriculum (England and Wales) Key Stage 2 in a coherent way. There are three books in the series, one for each of the attainment targets:

- ◆ Life Processes and Living Things
- ◆ Materials and their Properties
- ◆ Physical Processes

Materials and their Properties is divided into three chapters. Each begins with background information for the teacher, summarizing and explaining key concepts which pupils are expected to acquire.

After the background information you will find a chart listing the pupil activities, the resources needed, teaching/safety notes for each of the activities, and answers for the pupil pages. The answers are the writers' own results. In the complicated, but exciting world of science, these may be different from your results, but that does not make you wrong! Sometimes there will be small variations between the way in which you and the writers carried out the activities. This does not matter, and can make a good discussion point with pupils. The question 'why?' is a key part of science.

Pupils will need a pencil or pen for all the activities and additional sheets of paper are necessary for some. Other resources required are listed under 'Resources needed', and again at the top of each pupil page.

The 'Teaching/safety notes' give additional information and highlight areas where particular care is required. Before attempting any of the activities suggested, you should be fully conversant with the Association for Science Education's *Be Safe!* booklet and any guidelines laid down by your local authority/education department/ board of governors, etc.

The bulk of the book consists of pupil sheets that may be photocopied free of charge by the purchasing institution. The sheets provide a series of exciting investigations to reinforce the concepts in the pupils' minds. The activities closely adhere to QCA's Scheme of Work for Science and provide a practical, useful way for the teacher to administer the Scheme of Work.

To make the pupil sheets easy to use we have used logos along the left margin to flag the different types of text:

 Passages the pupil should read in order to find out more about the topic

 Investigations, experiments, puzzles, and other activities

 The pupil has to write an answer down

 Activities which stretch the pupil. Many require the use of reference books and/or CD-ROMs.

The contents page indicates which section of the National Curriculum Programme of Study is addressed on each pupil sheet.

Where practicable, you should attempt the activities yourself before introducing them to your pupils. You should also ensure that the equipment you intend to use is suitable for the activity/activities and the children using it.

We must emphasize that all activities should be carried out under teacher supervision. The publishers do not accept liability for any injury or damage howsoever caused arising from activities suggested in this publication.

No scheme can give teachers all the answers. However, we hope that this scheme will enable you to use your time where it can be spent most productively – namely helping individual pupils rather than doing repetitive planning and preparing worksheets.

We hope you and your pupils will enjoy **Project Science**.

To obtain a copy of *Be Safe!* contact the Association for Science Education, College Lane, Hatfield, Hertfordshire AL10 9AA.

Grouping and Classifying Materials

Background information

All the materials in the world around us are made from a limited number of chemical elements. These elements are listed in the periodic table, which shows them in order of their atomic number.

Metals are usually defined by their hardness, strength, conduction of heat and electricity, malleability and high melting points. If we consider strength, most pure metals, such as aluminium, iron and copper, are actually quite soft and are made stronger by adding other atoms. Iron, for example, is hardly ever used in its pure form but as a form of steel. Conduction in a material depends on whether or not there are 'free' electrons to carry the heat or electricity. An exception to the typical metal is mercury, which is liquid at room temperature.

Man-made and natural materials

More and more man-made **building** materials are being used instead of materials found naturally. This is because of the cost and convenience involved in both buying and using them. In house building, man-made brick, concrete and steel are used in preference to their natural counterparts – stone, granite and

Helpful words	
Periodic table	Sedimentary
Man-made	Metamorphic
Natural materials	Particles
Igneous	

sandstone. Man-made tiles and cladding replace slates and thatching. Even wood is being substituted by cheaper plywood, medium density fibreboard (MDF) or gyproc.

In the **textile** industry, man-made fibres have been around since 1930 when man-made nylon virtually replaced silk in the stocking market. The durability of man-made acrylic, viscose and polyester, for example, often make them better for certain purposes than natural fibres such as cotton, wool, flax, silk, mohair and cashmere.

Rocks can be one of three types: igneous, sedimentary or metamorphic. Igneous rock starts deep beneath the Earth's crust. As molten magma it pushes up through the crust, where it cools and solidifies. There are many different kinds of igneous rocks formed, depending on the composition of the magma and the way it cools and forms crystals. Examples of igneous rocks are

Rock type	Structure	Porous?	Hardness
Igneous	small grained	impervious to water	very hard
Sedimentary	loose grained	porous	soft
Metamorphic	layered appearance	impervious to water	hard

granite and basalt. Sedimentary rock is usually formed when rock of any type is weathered down into fine particles which are then redeposited under water and compacted. Limestone is the most common example of a sedimentary rock. Metamorphic rock can be igneous or sedimentary rock which has been subjected to high pressure and/or temperature so that its nature has changed. Marble is an example of a metamorphic rock formed from the change of limestone, while quartzite is formed from the change of sandstone.

All **soils** are composed of four basic components: mineral particles, organic matter, air and water. Mineral particles are the non-living skeleton of the soil and come from the decomposition of rocks. The organic matter (or humus) is a mixture of living organisms and dead, decomposed organisms, both animal and vegetable. Soil can be classified as anything from light to heavy depending on its make-up. Soil ideally should have plenty of nutrients

and organic matter and a sufficient quantity of lime. This would give it:
◆ a crumbly structure
◆ medium texture
◆ free drainage.

Its structure refers to the way the mineral particles are joined together – as clumps, plates or crumbs, for example. Texture refers to the proportion of different-sized materials. In light soil there are coarse particles like sand (90% sand, 10% silt and clay). In heavy soil there are fine particles like clay (55% sand and silt, 45% clay). Different soils suit different purposes.

Solids, liquids and gases

Matter can be divided into three states: **solids**, **liquids** and **gases**.

Solids (for example wood or glass) are defined as materials with a fixed shape and volume. Children are often unsure about materials such as sponge because it can be squashed into different shapes. Sponge is classified as a solid as the

Soil	Characteristics	Where used
Sandy	feels gritty good drainage easy to work	ideal for early crops but needs a lot of plant food because of good drainage
Clay	feels sticky when moist poor drainage hard to work	in industry (not suitable for crops as poor drainage causes waterlogging)

Grouping and Classifying Materials

definition of a solid is based on observing the material without any acting external forces. A solid cannot move or flow. The particles in the solid state are strongly bonded together, which prevents them from flowing.

Liquids (for example water or oil) are defined as materials with no fixed shape but a fixed volume. The particles in the liquid state have weak bonds between them, continually breaking and reforming, thus allowing the particles to flow.

Gases (for example oxygen or methane) are defined as having no fixed shape or volume. The particles in the gaseous state have no bonds between them and are therefore free to move at random.

Some ideas for further work

◆ Find out more about Mohs scale of hardness. Diamond is classified as 10 and talc is classified as 1.

◆ Study the materials used in a local playground. Make a list of the different materials, where they are used and what physical property makes them suitable for their use.

◆ Investigate the materials which are used to make items such as the soles of training shoes, bungee rope, cortex rain jackets (find out what cortex means), astroturf, bullet-proof glass, police body armour, polythene bags. Why are these materials used and what makes them so different?

◆ Look at the labels of clothes and classify them into man-made and natural materials.

◆ Make a list of clothes which are worn in the winter to keep warm. Find out why they help keep us warm (thickness of material, type of material and the design of the materials – many warm clothes are designed to trap air, which is a good heat insulator).

◆ How did Captain Scott hope to keep himself and his men warm on their trip to the South Pole?

◆ Use books or CD-ROMs to find out about Benjamin Franklin and his experiments with lightning conductors.

◆ Investigate the uses of gases and liquids in such things as air-bags in cars and hydraulic machinery.

◆ Design you own home, including furniture, using only locally available natural materials. Make a model of your new home.

Grouping and Classifying Materials

Activity	Answers	Resources needed	Teaching/ safety notes
Sheet 1 (page 16) Common materials	Answers could include: • scissors are made from steel because it is strong; • elastic band is made from rubber because it is easily stretched.	Various classroom objects	
Sheet 2 (page 17) Materials and properties	Metal Strong, hard, can be bent and conducts heat and electricity easily Plastic Flexible, is easily moulded and can burn when heated Fibre Flexible, burns easily and can be cut easily Ceramic Hard, brittle and heat resistant Glass Transparent, hard and brittle	Scissors Glue Card	
Sheet 3 (page 18) Hardness	The Plasticine should keep its shape more when dropped onto carpet and linoleum, but should be distorted more when dropped onto the hard surfaces, such as wood and tile.	Plasticine Ruler 4 floor coverings (such as carpet, wood, tile and llinoleum)	A piece of Plasticine was rolled into a ball with a diameter of 50 mm. The ball was then dropped onto each surface from a height of 100 cm and its height was then remeasured from the surface which it hit to the top. The thickness of the materials used should be the same to make a fair comparison. Layers can be used to increase thickness.
Sheet 4 (page 19) The rub test	• Carpet – fibres are rubbed off • Wood – easily scratched and dust is produced • Tile – not easily scratched and no dust. • Linoleum – easily scratched.	Sandpaper Block of wood 4 floor coverings (such as carpet, wood, tile and linoleum)	An additional activity to this test is to compare the effect on different types of wood (hard/soft, etc).
Sheet 5 (page 20) Stretchiness	The length of the leg of the tights will increase as the mass increases.	2 pairs of varied denier tights Ruler/measuring tape Masses (100 g – 1000 g)	Use one leg of the tights. Lighter weight tights should be more elastic. Children may find it easier to use a measuring tape for measuring.

Grouping and Classifying Materials

Activity	Answers	Resources needed	Teaching/ safety notes
Sheet 6 (page 21) Natural or man-made?	**Man-made** roof tiles brick plastic glass concrete bronze steel **Natural** slate stone wood cobble		Natural is defined as made from organic materials, not synthetic.
Sheet 7 (page 22) What is our school made of?	As above.		
Sheet 8 (page 23) Materials in homes	The builders used naturally occurring materials which they found in or around their natural environment.		
Sheet 9 (page 24) Magnetic materials	Magnetic: steel screw, iron pot Non-magnetic: the other items.	Strong magnet Selection of different materials	Most materials are not magnetic. Powerful magnets are normally made from man-made alloys such as alnico.
Sheet 10 (page 25) Turning a nail into a magnet	It is not really possible to make very strong magnets in this way and it is not possible to make any non-magnetic material into a permanent magnet in this way either.	Strong magnet Small nail Paper clips	The Earth generates its own magnetic field and if a small nail which has been magnetized in this way is floated in water on a small piece of wood then it is possible to use this to demonstrate how a compass works.
Sheet 11 (page 26) Keeping ice cubes cold	The aluminium foil and sponge sheeting will probably keep the ice cubes cold for longer.	Thermometer Ice cubes Bubble wrap Sponge sheeting Aluminium foil Polythene	
Sheet 12 (page 27) Keeping water warm	It was found that the bottle with no wrapping cooled down more quickly.	Thermometer 5 bottles of warm water Bubble wrap Sponge sheeting Aluminium foil Polythene	Take care with glass bottles. Take care with warm water.

Grouping and Classifying Materials

Activity	Answers	Resources needed	Teaching/ safety notes
Sheet 13 (page 28) Heat conductors and heat insulators	• Metal is a better conductor of heat than wood or plastic. The metal handle should feel the warmest at the top. • The pot has a plastic handle because plastic is a poor conductor of heat. • The pot has a metal bottom to conduct the heat from the ring of the cooker to the food. • The radiator is made of metal to conduct the heat from the water inside to the air outside. • The kettle is made of plastic to stop heat loss so that the water boils more quickly. Plastic is not a good conductor of electricity, making the kettle safer.	Bowl of hot water Metal ladle Wooden spoon Spatula with a plastic handle	Take care with hot water.
Sheet 14 (page 29) Conductors and insulators 1	• Conductors: aluminium, graphite, silver coin, iron nail, brass key, copper coin, metal pins on a plug, steel paper clips. • Insulators: plastic ruler, paper, card, plastic plug, cloth, thread, wool.	Battery in battery holder 3 wires Bulb Materials to test	Given a high enough voltage all materials will conduct. A good example of this is lightning travelling through air (an insulator). Take care with electricity.
Sheet 15 (page 30) Conductors and insulators 2	See above. In general metals usually are good conductors; non-metals are usually insulators.	Sheet 14	
Sheet 16 (page 31) Different rocks	The rocks suggested are all smooth, except sandstone, which is rough.	Selection of rocks Hand lens	Colours and patterns will vary.
Sheet 17 (page 32) Hardness of rocks	Rocks such as granite, marble, limestone and slate are all too hard to be scratched. Sandstone can be scratched, and chalk can be scratched easily.	Selection of rocks Hand lens Scissors Copper coin Protective goggles	The tip of a tungsten carbide drill bit could be used to scratch harder rocks. Wear protective goggles to protect the eyes.

Grouping and Classifying Materials

Activity	Answers	Resources needed	Teaching/ safety notes
Sheet 18 (page 33) Water absorbency of rocks	• The chalk should show the greatest increase in weight as it is absorbent. • Sandstone should show a smaller increase in weight. • In our experiment slate and marble showed a very small increase and granite and limestone no increase.	Selection of rocks Kitchen scales Bowl of water	
Sheet 19 (page 34) The water drop test	In our test chalk absorbed the water in 4 seconds and sandstone in 10 seconds. The water was still there after 5 minutes for marble, slate, granite and limestone.	Selection of rocks Timer Magnifying glass Water dropper	This presents a good opportunity to discuss why slate is often used to cover roofs and marble is sometimes used in bathrooms. Houses with sandstone walls can become damp.
Sheet 20 (page 35) Measuring volume	**Cylinder** **Volume** 1 10 cm^3 2 60 cm^3 3 90 cm^3 4 55 cm^3 5 100 cm^3 6 30 cm^3		If you look closely at the top of the water in the measuring cylinder you will see that it forms a curve. This curve is called a **meniscus** and is caused by the surface tension. The volume reading is taken from the bottom of the meniscus.
Sheet 21 (page 36) Water absorbency of soils	The sandy soil should allow more water to filter through than the clay soil.	Sandy soil Clay soil Filter paper Funnel Measuring jug Basin Measuring cylinder Timer	
Sheet 22 (page 37) Air in soil	The clay soil should absorb more water than the sandy soil. Clay soil has more air spaces. (Answers will depend on the types of soils used.)	Measuring cylinder Water jug Spoon 4 types of soil	

Grouping and Classifying Materials

Activity	Answers	Resources needed	Teaching/ safety notes
Sheet 23 (page 38) Solids and liquids	• Solids: butter, banana, pot, sponge, soap. • Liquids: milk, honey, cooking oil, water.	Scissors Glue Card	Liquids flow easily and take the shape of their containers. A liquid has a fixed volume (if temperature and pressure are kept constant). A liquid is smooth (not lumpy) and will be absorbed by porous materials such as sponges and paper towels.
Sheet 24 (page 39) Solids, liquids and shape	• Solids: golf ball, rubber, bottle, pencil, brick. • Liquids: water, orange juice, milk, rain.		Solids keep their shape (unless a force makes this change) and have a fixed volume (if temperature and pressure remain constant). A solid can be lumpy and will not fill up every space in its container. Solids are not absorbed by porous materials such as sponges and paper towels.
Sheet 25 (page 40) Measuring the volume of liquids	The volume remains the same.	Beaker Funnel Measuring cylinder Containers of different shapes and sizes	The shape of the liquid changes but its volume remains the same.
Sheet 26 (page 41) Trapped air and moving air	When the items are fully inflated their volume increases and they keep their shape better. The wind: • blows the wind surfer along • makes the flag flap • blows the umbrella away • holds the kite high up • turns the fan blades of the windmill • helps make the ocean waves.	Pump Beach ball Other inflatables	Air is a mixture of different gases. The most abundant gas in air is nitrogen which makes up 78% of air, oxygen making up 21%. The other 1% is made up of carbon dioxide (0.03%) and other gases, called noble gases, such as argon. Carbon dioxide contributes to the greenhouse effect.

Grouping and Classifying Materials

Activity	Answers	Resources needed	Teaching/ safety notes
Sheet 27 (page 42) Air bubbles	Bubbles of air are seen coming out of the sponge and sand. This is because there are spaces between the particles which are filled with air. When the water is added to the marbles it can be seen flowing into the air spaces between the marbles. It pushes out the air, which is seen rising to the surface as bubbles.	Sponge Bowl of water Jar Marbles Sand Jug of water	
Sheet 28 (page 43) Common gases	**Picture Gases** 1 steam 2 carbon dioxide 3 acetylene 4 hot air 5 natural gas 6 chlorine 7 hydrogen 8 helium 9 air		Gases do not have a fixed shape or volume and will spread out (diffuse) to completely fill and take the shape of their containers. Many gases, such as oxygen, nitrogen and carbon dioxide, are colourless. Coloured gases are normally very dangerous and poisonous.
Sheet 29 (page 44) Comparing solids and liquids	The liquid (water) flows easily into the containers and takes on their shape. The pebbles do not flow easily and do not take on the shape of their container completely.	Funnel Jug of water Plastic bottle Plastic bowl Plastic tub Pebbles	Very fine solids, such as flour, which are made from small lumps of solid do behave rather like liquids. However, each particle behaves like an individual solid. Gases flow easier than liquids. Gases are easier to squash than liquids.
Sheet 30 (page 45) Comparing liquids and gases	• The air flows best, followed by the water. • The balloon filled with air is easier to squash than the balloon filled with water.	Syringe Bowl of water Empty bowl 2 balloons Funnel Jug of water	
Sheet 31 (page 46) The perfume test	When the water bottle is opened it can not be smelled. When the perfume bottle is opened the perfume is smelled very quickly afterwards.	Bottle of water Bottle of perfume (plus lids)	The liquid perfume at the top of the bottle evaporates into a vapour (gas). As a vapour, it spreads through the air (diffuses).

Common materials

Materials are often chosen to make objects because of their particular properties. A chair can be made from wood because the wood is not too cold to sit on. A window is made from glass because glass is transparent.

Pick some objects from around the classroom. Which materials are they mostly made from? Why have these materials been chosen?

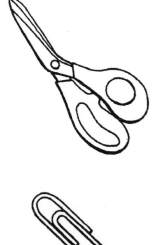

Object	From which material is it mostly made?	Why is this material used?
Chair	It is made mostly from wood.	Wood is not too cold to sit on.

Materials and properties

You need: scissors, glue and card.

Activity

◆ Cut out and match the materials with the words or phrases which best describe their properties.

◆ Glue them onto a piece of card.

Materials	Properties
Metals	Flexible, burns easily and can be cut easily
Plastic	Hard, brittle and heat resistant
Fibre	Strong, hard, can be bent and conducts heat and electricity easily
Ceramic	Transparent, hard and brittle
Glass	Flexible, is easily moulded and can burn when heated

Hardness

You need: Plasticine, a ruler and 4 floor coverings
(such as carpet, wood, tile and linoleum).

 Activity Let's investigate the hardness of different floor coverings. Drop a ball of Plasticine onto a sample of floor covering and draw how much the Plasticine is distorted.

Remember to drop the Plasticine from the same height. Make sure the floor coverings are all of the same thickness.

Floor material	How much is the Plasticine distorted?
Carpet	
Wood	
Tile	
Linoleum	

The rub test

You need: sandpaper, a block of wood and 4 floor coverings (such as carpet, wood, tile and linoleum).

 Activity Let's investigate how hard-wearing a floor covering is.

Wrap a piece of sandpaper around a block of wood. Rub each of the floor coverings in turn with the block. Describe what happens to the covering.

Floor material	How hard wearing is it?
Carpet	
Wood	
Tile	
Linoleum	

Stretchiness

You need: 2 pairs of tights, a ruler or measuring tape and 100 g to 1000 g masses.

 Activity

Let's compare how elastic (how much they stretch) two different makes of tights are by adding 100 g masses inside them.

Measure the length of the tights each time you add a 100 g mass.

Mass added to tights	Length of the first pair of tights	Length of the second pair of tights
no mass		
100 g		
200 g		
300 g		
400 g		
500 g		
600 g		
700 g		
800 g		
900 g		
1000 g		

 Answer

Which pair of tights is the most elastic?

Natural or man-made?

 Activity Some materials used for building are **natural** and some are **man-made**.

Look at the pictures below. Discuss the materials you think may have been used to build each one.

Part of building	Natural or man-made?
Roof	
House walls	
Door	
Front step	
Window	
Chimney pot	

Part of building	Natural or man-made?
Roof	
Church walls	
Doors	
Path	

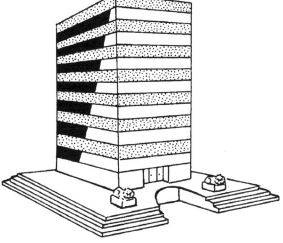

Part of building	Natural or man-made?
Roof	
Walls	
Windows	
Doors	
Statues	
Stair terrace	

What is our school made of?

 Find out which materials have been used to make the outside of your school building(s) and grounds.

Part of the school	Material from which it is mostly made	Is it a natural or man-made material?
Roof		
Walls of the building		
Windows		
Doors		
Steps or stairs		
Benches or tables		
Fence or wall of playground		

Materials in homes

Read   Around the world people's homes are designed to suit their climate. The homes are often made from materials which are found in the area where the people live.

Activity   Find out why people in the past built homes like these.

1 Igloo made of blocks of snow and ice	
2 Log cabin with a stone chimney	
3 North American teepee covered in buffalo skins	
4 Crofter's cottage with grass roof and stone walls	
5 Desert tent made out of goat skin	
6 Kalahari hut made with mud walls and thatched roof	

Magnetic materials

You need: a strong magnet and a selection of
different materials (see below).

 Read If a material is attracted to a magnet, then it
is magnetic. Most materials are not
magnetic but some are.

 Activity Find out which of the materials below are
magnetic and which are not. Tick the box if
they are magnetic.

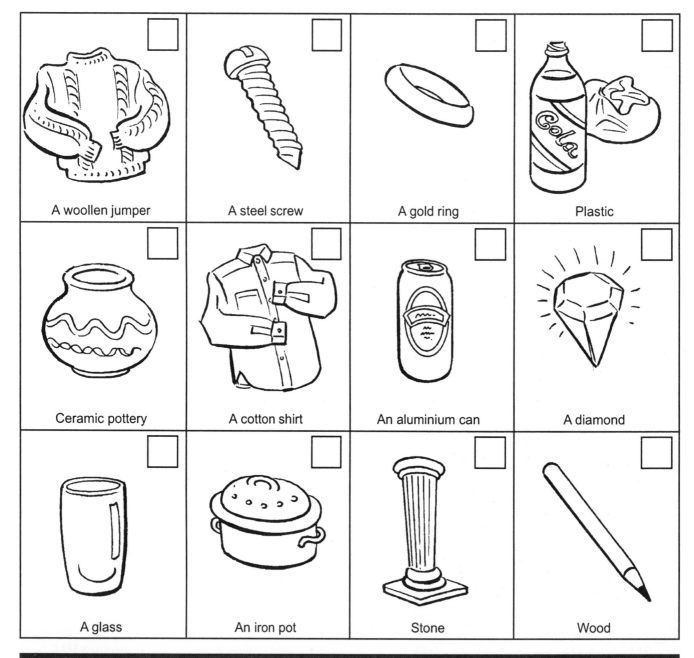

A woollen jumper	A steel screw	A gold ring	Plastic
Ceramic pottery	A cotton shirt	An aluminium can	A diamond
A glass	An iron pot	Stone	Wood

Turning a nail into a magnet

You need: a strong magnet, a small nail and some paper clips.

 Activity

◆ Make a magnetic material like a steel nail into a magnet by stroking it from head to tip with a bar magnet.

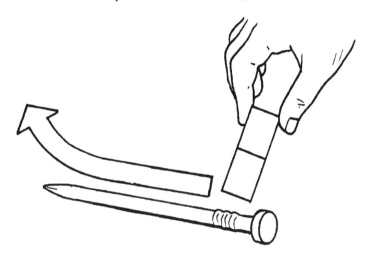

◆ It is important that you always move the magnet is the same direction.

◆ Test the strength of your new magnet by finding out how many paper clips it can pick up.

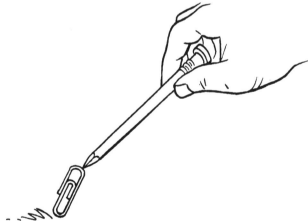

 Look further

Find out if you can make any other materials into magnets.

Keeping ice cubes cold

You need: a thermometer, ice cubes, bubble wrap, sponge sheeting, aluminium foil and polythene.

Read

If an ice cube is left in a room it will absorb heat from the air around it and begin to melt. This is because the air around the ice cube is at a higher temperature (warmer) than the ice cube. The ice cube heats up and begins to melt.

Activity

Use a thermometer to measure the temperature of an ice cube and the temperature of the air in the room.

Temperature of the ice cube	
Temperature of the air in the room	

Look further

You could investigate whether wrapping ice cubes in different materials helps keep them cold.

◆ Wrap some ice cubes in each of the materials.

◆ Unwrap the ice cubes every 15 minutes and draw what you see.

	Bubble wrap	**Sponge**	**Aluminium foil**	**Polythene**
What it looks like after 15 minutes				
What it looks like after 30 minutes				

Keeping water warm

You need: a thermometer, 5 bottles of warm water, bubble wrap, sponge sheeting, aluminium foil and polythene.

 Read
We wear different types of clothes in different weather. If it is cold we wear clothes which will keep us warm. Clothes keep us warm by stopping the heat from our bodies escaping.

 Activity
Use a thermometer to measure the temperature of the water from the tap. When a bottle is filled with warm water, the water quickly cools down as it loses heat.

Let's find out which material is best at keeping the water the warmest for the longest time. Record the temperature changes of the water in the table below.

Material	Temperature at the start	After 5 mins	After 10 mins	After 15 mins	After 20 mins	After 25 mins
No wrapping						
Bubble wrap						
Sponge						
Aluminium foil						
Polythene						

Materials and their Properties

Heat conductors and heat insulators

You need: a bowl of hot water, a metal ladle, a
wooden spoon and a spatula with a plastic handle.

Activity Ask your teacher to put the utensils in the hot water.

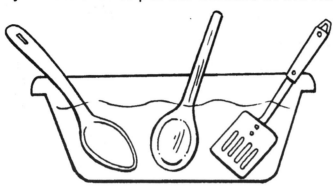

After five to ten minutes ask your teacher if you can feel the handles of each
utensil.

Answer How warm are each of the handles?

Look further Find out why these objects, or parts of them, are made from the
materials shown.

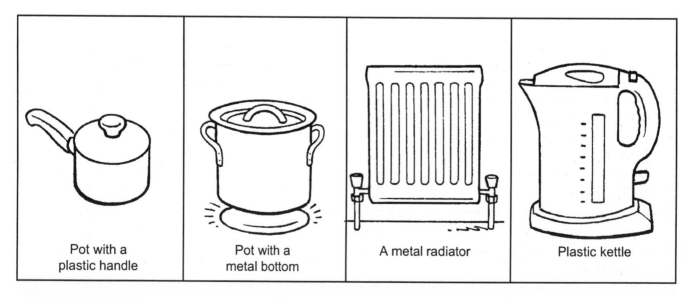

| Pot with a plastic handle | Pot with a metal bottom | A metal radiator | Plastic kettle |

Conductors and insulators 1

You need: a battery, 3 wires, a bulb and some
materials to test.

 Activity Let's find out which materials allow electricity to pass through them.

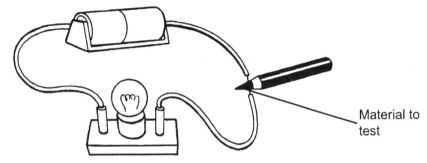

Material to
test

◆ Set up a circuit
like this.

◆ Place the materials in the gap in turn and watch what happens. (Use your own
choice of materials if you wish.)

◆ Tick the materials which allow electricity to pass through them.

◆ If the bulb lights, the material is a conductor. If the bulb does not light, then the
material is an insulator.

Plastic ruler	Aluminium can	Paper	Graphite	Silver coin
Iron nail	Card	Brass key	Plastic	Cloth
Thread	Copper coin	Wool	Metal	Steel paper clip

 Read Materials which allow electricity to pass through them are called
conductors. Materials which do not allow electricity to pass through
them are called **insulators**.

Conductors and insulators 2

You need: Sheet 14.

Activity Put the materials you tested in the correct column.

Conductor	Insulator

Answer What do you notice about the materials which do allow electricity to pass through them?

What do you notice about the materials which do **not** allow electricity to pass through them?

Different rocks

You need: a selection of rocks (such as chalk, limestone, marble, granite, slate and sandstone) and a hand lens.

Activity

◆ Use a hand lens to look closely at each rock.

◆ Use your observations to complete the table.

Rock	Colour(s)	Texture (rough or smooth)	Draw any patterns in the rock
Chalk			
Limestone			
Marble			
Granite			
Slate			
Sandstone			

Materials and their Properties

Hardness of rocks

You need: a selection of rocks (such as chalk, limestone, marble, granite, slate and sandstone), a hand lens, scissors, a copper coin, protective goggles.

Read A German mineralogist called Friedrich Mohs measured the hardness of rocks by seeing how easy it was to scratch them. The Mohs scale is named after him. In the Mohs scale of hardness the hardest rock has a value of 10 and the softest rock has a value of 1.

Activity ◆ Use a copper coin to find how easy (or difficult) it is to scratch the different rocks.

◆ Examine the scratches with a hand lens.

◆ Cut out the pictures of the rocks and use the results from your scratch test to arrange them into an order of hardness.

Take care! Make sure that particles of rock do not get into your eyes!

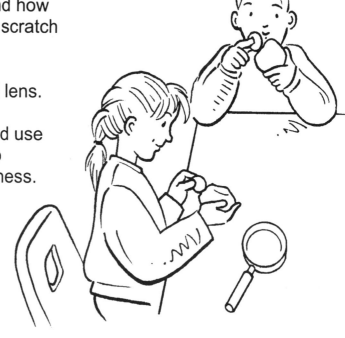

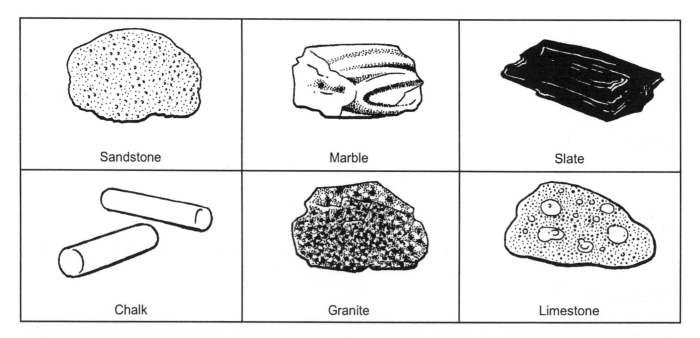

Sandstone	Marble	Slate
Chalk	Granite	Limestone

Water absorbency of rocks

You need: a selection of rocks (such as chalk, limestone, marble, granite, slate and sandstone), kitchen scales and a bowl of water.

 Activity Some materials are absorbent. They soak up water.

Let's investigate how much water each rock absorbs.

Weigh them when they are dry. Soak them overnight in water and weigh them again the following day.

Rock	Weight when dry	Weight after being soaked	Increase in weight
Chalk	grams	grams	grams
Limestone	grams	grams	grams
Marble	grams	grams	grams
Granite	grams	grams	grams
Slate	grams	grams	grams
Sandstone	grams	grams	grams

 Answer Is this a fair test to find out which type of rock is the most absorbent?

Why do you think so?

The water drop test

You need: a selection of rocks (such as chalk, limestone, marble, granite, slate and sandstone), a timer, a magnifying glass and a water dropper.

 Activity Let's investigate how long it takes different rocks to absorb a water drop. Work in pairs.

◆ Add a droplet of water to a sample of rock.

◆ Time how long it takes for the water droplet to disappear (some rocks may not absorb the water drop).

◆ Use the results from your investigation to fill in the table.

	Chalk	Limestone	Marble	Granite	Slate	Sandstone
Time taken to absorb the water droplet						

 Answer Which rocks are the best at absorbing water?

Which are the worst?

Measuring volume

 Activity What is the volume of water in each of the measuring cylinders?

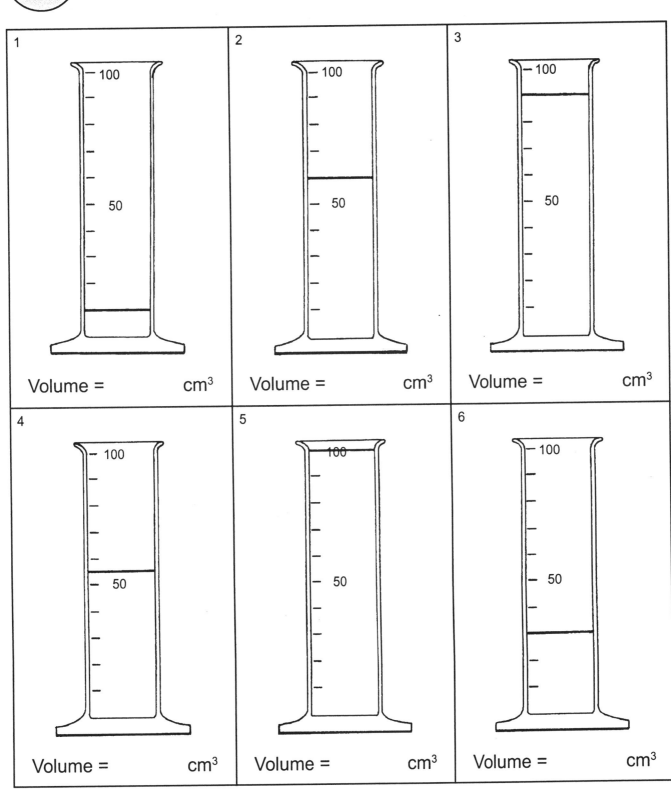

1

Volume =   cm³

2

Volume =   cm³

3

Volume =   cm³

4

Volume =   cm³

5

Volume =   cm³

6

Volume =   cm³

Water absorbency of soils

You need: some sandy soil, some clay soil, filter paper, a funnel, a measuring jug, a basin, a measuring cylinder and a timer.

◆ Fold some filter paper and place it in the funnel. (This stops most of the soil from running into the measuring cylinder.)

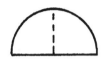 

◆ Place the funnel in the measuring cylinder. Put some of the sandy soil into the funnel.

◆ Fill the funnel to the top of the filter paper with water.

◆ Measure how much water flows through the soil in 20 seconds.

◆ Repeat with the clay soil.

	Sandy soil	Clay soil
Volume of water which flowed through in 20 seconds		

Remember to use the same amount of soil each time and to fill the funnel with water.

Can you explain why you got different volumes of water?

Air in soil

You need: a measuring cylinder, a water jug, a spoon and 4 different types of soil (such as sandy, clay, peat and loam).

 Read The spaces between soil particles contain air. This air is needed by the roots of plants and animals, such as worms, which live in the soil. The air spaces also make it easier for animals to burrow through the soil.

When water is added to dry soil the water level drops as it soaks into the soil and pushes out the air. Soil with lots of air spaces soaks up the most water.

 Activity Let's investigate which type of soil contains the most air spaces.

◆ Put 50 cm³ of the first soil into a measuring cylinder (the soil must be dry).

◆ Fill the measuring cylinder with water and then leave it for one hour. Repeat with the other soils.

◆ The drop of the water level shows the volume of air the soil contained.

	Sandy	**Clay**	**Peat**	**Loam**
Amount of water absorbed				

 Answer Which type of soil has the most air spaces between the particles?

Solids and liquids

You need: scissors, glue and card.

◆ Cut out and sort the things below into solids and liquids.

◆ Glue the solids onto one piece of card and the liquids onto another.

| Milk | Honey | Butter |

| Banana | Cooking pot | Cooking oil |

| Sponge | Water | Soap |

Solids, liquids and shape

Read Solid things keep their shape unless they are **forced** to change.

Liquids pour easily and take the shape of their containers without being forced to do so.

Activity Which of the pictures below show solids and which show liquids? Put a tick next to the solids.

Golf ball ☐	Water from a tap ☐	Orange juice ☐
Rubber ☐	Milk ☐	Bottle ☐
Pencil ☐	Rain ☐	Brick ☐

Answer The solid things are the...

The liquid things are the...

Measuring the volume of liquids

You need: a beaker, a funnel, a measuring cylinder and containers of different shapes and sizes.

 Read When a liquid is poured into a container the liquid flows and takes on the shape of the container.

 Activity Let's investigate whether the volume of water changes when it is poured into containers of different shapes and sizes.

◆ Use a beaker to pour the same amount of water into each container.

◆ Use a funnel to empty the water into a measuring cylinder.

◆ Measure the volume of the water in the cylinder.

Remember, you must use the same beaker filled to the same level each time.

Flask	Tea pot	Bowl
Volume = cm³	Volume = cm³	Volume = cm³
Yogurt carton	Washing-up liquid bottle	Small watering can
Volume = cm³	Volume = cm³	Volume = cm³

Trapped air and moving air

You need: a pump, a beach ball, other inflatables (such as a bicycle tyre, an air bed or a dinghy).

 ◆ Use a pump or your lungs to blow up a beach ball. Feel what happens to the beach ball as you pump or blow more air into it.

◆ Describe what the items below feel like when there is no air in them and then when they are fully inflated with air.

Beach ball	Bicycle tyre	Air bed or dinghy

 The air in the objects is trapped. **Trapped air** can be useful to keep things like footballs inflated and rigid.

Use the pictures below to describe some of the effects of **moving air**.

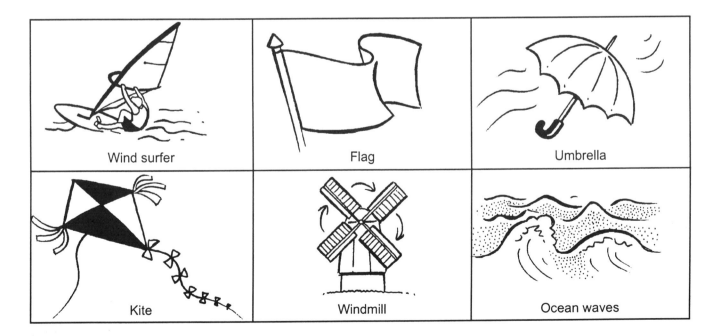

Wind surfer	Flag	Umbrella
Kite	Windmill	Ocean waves

Materials and their Properties

Air bubbles

You need: a sponge, a bowl of water, a jar, some
marbles, some sand in a bowl and a jug of water.

◆ Put a dry sponge into a bowl of water and then give the sponge a
squeeze.

What do you see happening?

◆ Pour some water into a jar containing marbles.

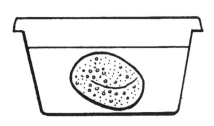

What do you see happening?

◆ Pour some water onto some sand in a bowl.

What do you see happening?

Explain your observations from the three activities above.

© M Abraitis, A Deighan, B Gallagher, B Smith & M Toner

Common gases

 Activity Use books and/or CD-ROMs to find out the names of the gases being used in the pictures below.

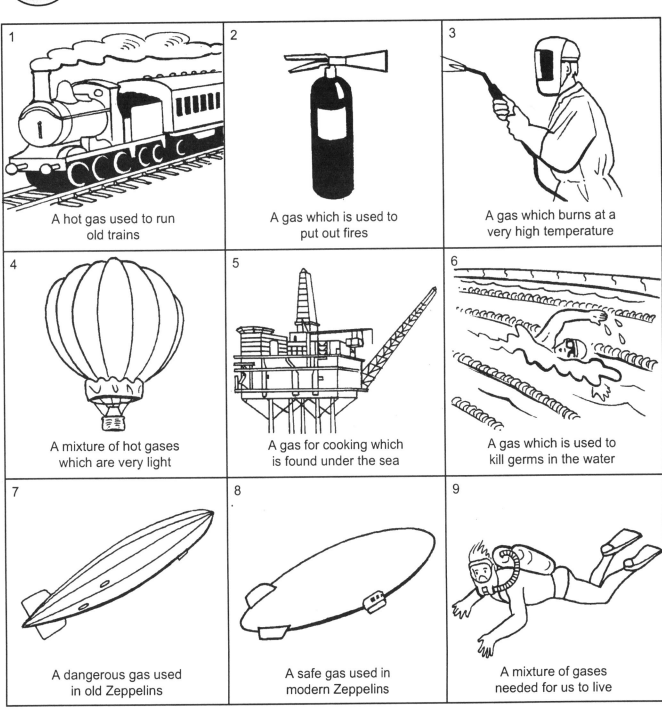

1 A hot gas used to run old trains

2 A gas which is used to put out fires

3 A gas which burns at a very high temperature

4 A mixture of hot gases which are very light

5 A gas for cooking which is found under the sea

6 A gas which is used to kill germs in the water

7 A dangerous gas used in old Zeppelins

8 A safe gas used in modern Zeppelins

9 A mixture of gases needed for us to live

steam	hydrogen	helium
air	carbon dioxide	hot air
chlorine	acetylene	natural gas

Materials and their Properties

Comparing solids and liquids

You need: a funnel, a jug of water, a plastic bottle,
a bowl, a tub and some pebbles.

◆ Pour some water from the jug into the plastic bottle. Use the funnel
to help you.

◆ Then pour the water from the bottle into the bowl and then finally into the tub.

What can you say about the way the water (liquid) changes shape and
the way it flows?

◆ Now try the experiment using pebbles instead of water.

What can you say about the way the pebbles (solid) change shape
and the way they flow?

Comparing liquids and gases

You need: a syringe (without the needle), a bowl of sand, a bowl of water, an empty bowl, 2 balloons, a funnel and a jug of water.

 Activity

◆ Fill the syringe with air and then empty the air out. Repeat this several times.

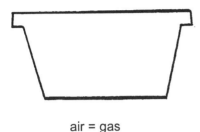

air = gas

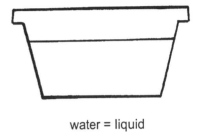

water = liquid

 Answer

Which of the three substances flowed best: the gas (air) or the liquid (water)?

Which flowed least well?

 Activity

◆ Fill one balloon with air and another balloon with water. Tie them both securely.

◆ Squash each of the balloons gently, observing how it feels.

 Answer

Which of the two balloons changes shape more easily?

Can you explain why?

The perfume test

You need: a bottle of water and a bottle of perfume, both with lids.

◆ Place a closed bottle of perfume and a closed bottle of water a short distance away from you.

◆ Ask someone to open the bottle of water. Wait a few moments, then sniff the air.

◆ Now ask someone to open the bottle of perfume. Wait a few moments, then sniff the air.

What happens when the bottle of water is opened?

What happens when the bottle of perfume is opened?

Use your observations from the last series of activities to write a note on the differences between solids, liquids and gases. Think of the way they flow, retain their shape and volume, and how they are released into the air.

Changing Materials

Background information

Changes to materials can be **physical** or **chemical**. A physical change like squashing can usually be reversed, whereas a chemical change like burning cannot be reversed.

The **water cycle** is an example of a process which makes use of reversible changes. Water can exist in three states, namely ice, water and steam. It can change to each of the three states by the reversible processes of melting, freezing, condensing and evaporating. Water, like energy, cannot be lost or created on the Earth's surface. It just moves round the cycle, changing from one state to another. The vast majority (97%) of the water in the cycle comes from the Earth's seas and oceans. The remaining water is fresh water from the glaciers and ice sheets, or from underground.

Some ideas for further work

◆ Use books and/or CD-ROMs to find out what 'the greenhouse effect' is and what its impact on the ice at the North and South Poles will be.

Helpful words	
Dissolving	Evaporating
Melting	Reversible changes
Condensing	Non-reversible
Freezing	changes

◆ Tour the school and make a list of areas where non-reversible changes are taking place. Look at railings rusting, wood rotting, food cooking and gas, coal and oil burning.

◆ Investigate how materials can be adapted to improve their hardness and/ or rigidity. Think about plywood and corrugated iron, for example. Experiment with different materials such as card and cloth.

◆ Devise ways of allowing solids, liquids and gases to move more easily. Think about heating (chocolate, lava, wax) and crushing (lump plaster, sugar lumps).

Changing Materials

Activity	Answers	Resources needed	Teaching/ safety notes
Sheet 1 (page 55) Observing mixtures	• Salt and sugar dissolve and the water remains transparent. • Flour, coffee, powder paint and chalk colour the water. The flour and chalk settle on the bottom. • Sand and beads or marbles do not dissolve and sink to the bottom of the water.	9 beakers Spoon 9 different solids	Water is a good solvent and many substances can be dissolved in it. Some materials, such as flour, do not dissolve in water but, because of their tiny particles, float in the water and colour it. This is called a suspension. If left long enough the flour will sink to the bottom.
Sheet 2 (page 56) Heating water	• The water on the filter paper in a warm place will evaporate the fastest. • The water on the filter paper in a cool place will evaporate the slowest.	3 pieces of filter paper Water dropper Timer	The boiling temperature of water is 100 ºC. The average temperature of the water from the dropper will be much lower. A percentage of water particles will have a temperature above the average value and it is these particles which will evaporate. This is why puddles outside can evaporate even in fairly low temperatures. Hold the paper up to the light to tell if it is still wet.
Sheet 3 (page 57) Steam	• When steam cools down on a cold surface (eg a window) it **condenses** to form **water**. • When water vapour from our breath cools down on a cold surface it **condenses** to form **water**.	Kettle Small glass mirror	Steam has a lot more heat energy than boiling water. Consequently a burn from steam is more severe than one from boiling water. Children could be asked to explain why they see water on mirrors and water taps when a hot bath is being run.
Sheet 4 (page 58) Heating and cooling materials	The four solids melt. The order in which they melt may differ depending on what materials are used. In our case the order was ice, jelly (small cube), wax (from a candle) and then chocolate.	Kettle 4 test tubes Jelly Wax Chocolate Ice Kitchen scales Beaker	Test tubes help to demonstrate that the melted materials flow inside the container. When the materials freeze (solidify) then they freeze into the same shape as the bottom of the test tube.

Changing Materials

Activity	Answers	Resources needed	Teaching/ safety notes
Sheet 5 (page 59) Change of state	Changes of state by heating and cooling:	Scissors Glue Card	
Sheet 6 (page 60) Does it change back?	• Changes back when cooled: chocolate, gold, water, hot wax. • Does not change back when cooled: dough, egg, bread, cake mix and clay.		
Sheet 7 (page 61) Thermometer readings	**Thermometer Temperature** 1 40 °C 2 70 °C 3 10 °C 4 60 °C 5 100 °C 6 55 °C		Temperature is the measurement of how hot or cold something is. When a thermometer is used to measure how hot something is, the heat from the object flows to the liquid inside the thermometer, causing it to expand. When a thermometer is used to measure how cold something is, the heat flows from the liquid in the thermometer to the object, causing the liquid to contract.
Sheet 8 (page 62) Measuring temperature	Ruler – length Kitchen scales – weight Timer – time Thermometer – temperature	Thermometer Beaker of water Tap water Hot drink	Take care with the hot drink.
Sheet 9 (page 63) Reversible changes	• The dissolved salt in the water is left behind on the dish after all the water has evaporated. • Dissolving salt in water can be reversed.	Salt Spoon Beaker Plate (large, flat)	20 cm^3 of water with one teaspoon of salt dissolved in it was found to evaporate in two days when placed above a radiator.

Changing Materials

Activity	Answers	Resources needed	Teaching/ safety notes
Sheet 10 (page 64) Dissolving and stirring	• The sugar which is added to the water and is not stirred will sink and settle at the bottom. • The sugar which is added to the water and then stirred will dissolve quickly. • People stir their tea after adding sugar to it to dissolve the sugar.	Measuring cylinder Sugar granules Teaspoon 2 beakers	Stirring the water helps the water and sugar particles to mix more quickly and so speeds up the dissolving.
Sheet 11 (page 65) Dissolving and temperature	The sugar dissolves more quickly in the warm water. The temperature does affect how quickly the sugar dissolves. The higher the temperature, the more quickly the sugar will dissolve.	Measuring cylinder Thermometer Sugar granules Teaspoon 2 beakers	The higher the temperature of a liquid, the more quickly the particles of the liquid will move around. This speeds up the mixing of the sugar and water particles, helping the dissolving process. Be careful with hot water!
Sheet 12 (page 66) Dissolving and particle size	The caster sugar will dissolve the fastest, the sugar lumps will be the slowest.	Measuring cylinder Teaspoon Sugar lumps Granulated sugar Caster sugar 3 beakers Timer	An electronic balance could be used to weigh three equal masses of sugar to make the comparisons fairer and more accurate.
Sheet 13 (page 67) Melting	The water temperature will drop when the ice is added. The temperature will then rise towards the temperature of the room.	Glass Ice Thermometer	Heat flows from areas of high temperature to areas of lower temperature. The greater the temperature difference then the quicker the heat will flow. As the water loses heat to the ice its temperature will drop. If the water is warm (a high temperature) then the ice will melt quickly.
Sheet 14 (page 68) Melting and heat sources	Rock – volcano Wax candle – small flame Ice cream – the Sun Steel beam – furnace		Both a high temperature and a lot of heat energy are required to melt a rock and a steel beam.

Changing Materials

Activity	Answers	Resources needed	Teaching/ safety notes
Sheet 15 (page 69) Boiling	Water will boil at 100 °C.		Only pure water (distilled) will boil at 100 °C. Every chemical has its own unique freezing and boiling temperatures. This property is put to good use in chemistry to distil and separate mixtures such as crude oil. The Celsius scale is based on the freezing and boiling points of pure water, 0 °C and 100 °C.
Sheet 16 (page 70) Condensing	Water droplets form on the outside of the glass.	Ice Glass with a lid	At any time about 0.001% (13,000 cubic kilometres) of the total water on the Earth's surface is contained in the atmosphere.

Sheet 17 (page 71) Freezing	Water will freeze at 0 °C.
	
	The values below are only a guide:
	At the start 20 °C
	After 5 mins 15 °C
	        10 mins 10 °C
	        15 mins 7 °C
	        20 mins 6 °C
	        25 mins 5 °C
	        30 mins 4 °C
		Glass
		Ice
		Thermometer
		Fluffy towel
			100 cm^3 of water from the cold tap was allowed to sit in the room overnight to reach room temperature.
			
			The glass of water was placed in a small freezer bag and 18 standard ice cubes were placed between the bag and the glass.
			
			An elastic band was used to hold the bag tightly around the glass and a towel was then wrapped around the glass and bag to reduce the amount of ice melted by the heat in the room.

Sheet 18 (page 72) Evaporating	• The puddles get smaller because the water is evaporating. The more heat the water absorbs from the Sun, the quicker it will evaporate. • The wet hand print will eventually disappear as the water evaporates.	Kitchen towel	The average temperature of the water in the puddle will be below the 100 °C boiling point of water. A small percentage of the water particles will be at 100 °C and this is why the puddle begins to evaporate.

Changing Materials

Activity	Answers	Resources needed	Teaching/ safety notes
Sheet 19 (page 73) From liquid to gas	The perfume is a **liquid**. Some of it has **evaporated** and made a **gas**, which has travelled to me. I can smell it when it enters my **nose**.	Perfume Saucer	
Sheet 20 (page 74) Evaporation and air flow	The water will evaporate much faster when air is blown over it.	2 pieces of filter paper Water dropper Timer Hairdryer	
Sheet 21 (page 75) The plate and bowl test	The water in the dinner plate evaporates first followed by the water in the bowl. The water in the cylinder will take a long time to evaporate.	Measuring cylinder Dinner plate Bowl Food colouring	Increasing surface area speeds up evaporation. With a large surface area more water particles are on the surface (this is where they evaporate from) and the water has a larger surface from which it can absorb heat from the air in the room.
Sheet 22 (pages 76 and 77) The water cycle	• When the Sun shines on the water in the sea some water evaporates into water vapour and floats off up into the sky. • The water vapour becomes cold as it rises into the sky and condenses into small water droplets to form rain. • The clouds are blown over hills where the small water droplets cool down and form raindrops. • The rain falls down from the sky onto the Earth.	Scissors Glue Card Resource sheet	Around 0.35 million cubic kilometres of water is evaporated from the sea by the Sun each year. Most of the water falls back to the sea as rain (0.32 million cubic kilometres) and 0.11 million cubic kilometres falls on the land as rain each year. Some water is also evaporated from the land.
Sheet 23 (page 78) Non-reversible changes	• Reversible changes: ice melting, clothes drying. • Non-reversible changes: egg frying, cake baking, paint drying, match burning.		

Changing Materials

Activity	Answers	Resources needed	Teaching/ safety notes
Sheet 24 (page 79) Rusting nails	**Rusts the most quickly:** • nail in salt water • nail in water • nail in air • nail coated in grease.	Transparent plastic cups New, blunted nails Salt Grease	Tie a piece of thread around the nail so that it can be pulled out and inspected when required. For rusting to happen, oxygen and water must be present. The iron first reacts with the oxygen in the air to form hydrated iron oxide which is commonly known as rust. This rusting occurs faster if there is salt or other impurities present. The nail coated in grease does not rust because neither oxygen nor water can get to the nail through the grease. Covering iron railings with paint prevents them from rusting by stopping both oxygen and water getting to the iron underneath.
Sheet 25 (page 80) What changes	• Andrews salts and water – a gas is given off. • Plaster of Paris and water – a new substance is formed. • Petrol from a lighter – heat and light are given off. • Vinegar and chalk – a gas is given off. • Gas from a cooker – heat and light are given off. • Lemon juice and washing soda – a gas is given off.	6 beakers Andrews salts Plaster of Paris Lighter Vinegar Bicarbonate of soda Lemon juice Washing soda	Washing crystals (sodium carbonate) were used. Please note that washing soda is classified as an irritant. Read the Association for Science Education's booklet *Be Safe!* and always take care with chemicals.

Changing Materials

Activity	Answers	Resources needed	Teaching/ safety notes
Sheet 26 (page 81) Protecting fire fighters	The fire fighter wears special clothing and uses breathing apparatus. explosive flammable corrosive (burns) poisonous (toxic)		
Sheet 27 (page 82) Word search	1 burning 2 steam 3 melted 4 condensation 5 evaporate 6 dissolving 7 chemical 8 moving air 9 boils 10 thermometer		

Observing mixtures

You need: 9 beakers, a spoon and 9 different solids (such as salt, coffee, sugar, flour, powder paint, chalk, sand, glass beads or marbles, and plaster of Paris).

 Activity Add nine different solids to beakers of water and stir them. Wait a few moments and then record what happens in the spaces below.

Salt	Coffee	Sugar
Flour	**Powder paint**	**Chalk**
Sand	**Beads or marbles**	**Plaster of Paris**

Heating water

You need: 3 pieces of filter paper, a water dropper and a timer.

Read When water is heated it turns into a gas called **steam** and floats off up into the air. This is called **evaporation**.

All the water from a boiling pot of potatoes will evaporate if the heat is not turned off.

Activity Let's investigate whether temperature affects how quickly water evaporates from pieces of filter paper.

◆ Put five drops of water on three different filter papers.

◆ Put one of the filter papers in a warm place, such as over a radiator. Put one in a cool place, such as a fridge. Leave one on your desk.

◆ Time how long it takes for the water to evaporate from each of the filter papers.

Filter paper	Time taken for the water to evaporate
In a warm place	
In a cool place	
On your desk	

Answer Does temperature affect how long it takes for water to evaporate?

Steam

You need: a kettle and a small glass mirror.

 Activity Watch as your teacher evaporates some water from a kettle in front of a cold window.

 Answer Write down what happens to the hot steam when it reaches the cold window.

 Activity Breathe on a small mirror or cold window and observe what happens.

Useful words
condenses
water

 Answer

When steam cools down on a cold surface it _____

to form_____.

When water vapour from our breath cools down on a cold surface

it _____ to form _____.

Heating and cooling materials

You need: a kettle, four test tubes, jelly, wax, chocolate, ice, kitchen scales and a beaker.

◆ Use kitchen scales to weigh equal quantities of jelly, wax, chocolate and ice and then place each into a test tube.

◆ Ask your teacher to place the test tubes containing the four different solids into a beaker of hot water and watch carefully.

Useful words
Melt
Freeze

Describe what happens to each of the different solids.

Ask your teacher to put the four melted materials in a cool place overnight.

Describe what happens to each of the different liquids.

Change of state

You need: scissors, glue and card.

 When a material like water evaporates into steam, it is called a **change of state**. When steam condenses into water, this is another change of state.

 Cut out the diagrams and words below and glue them onto card showing how a material like water can change state when it is heated or cooled.

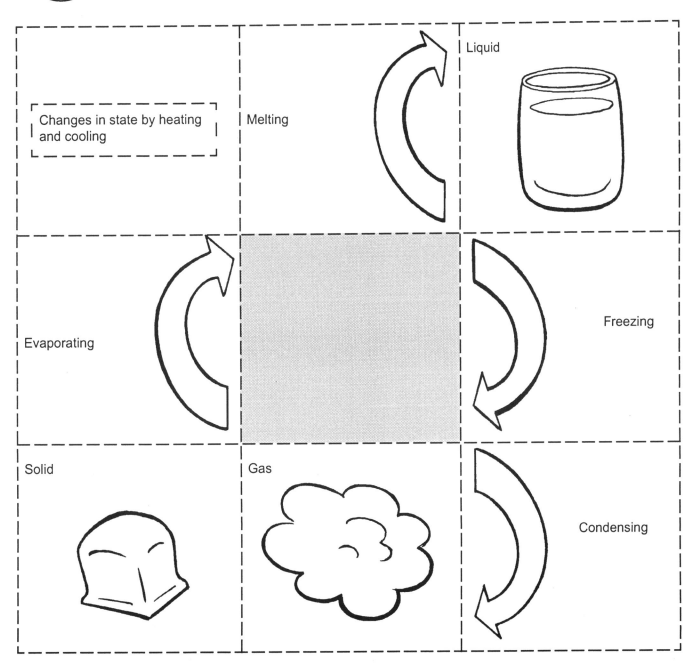

Changes in state by heating and cooling

Melting

Liquid

Evaporating

Freezing

Solid

Gas

Condensing

Does it change back?

Activity The pictures below show some materials being heated. Cut out each of the pictures and arrange them into two groups: things which change back when cooled and things which do not change back.

Chocolate being
heated in a pot

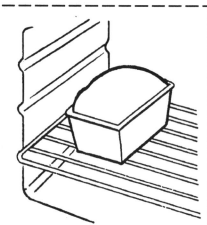

Dough being heated in
an oven

A raw egg being heated
in a frying pan

Gold being heated in a
furnace

Water being heated in
a kettle

Bread being heated in a
toaster

Cake mix being heated
in an oven

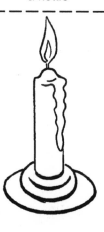

Hot wax running down
the side of a candle

Clay being heated
in a kiln

Thermometer readings

 Activity What are the temperature readings on the thermometers below?

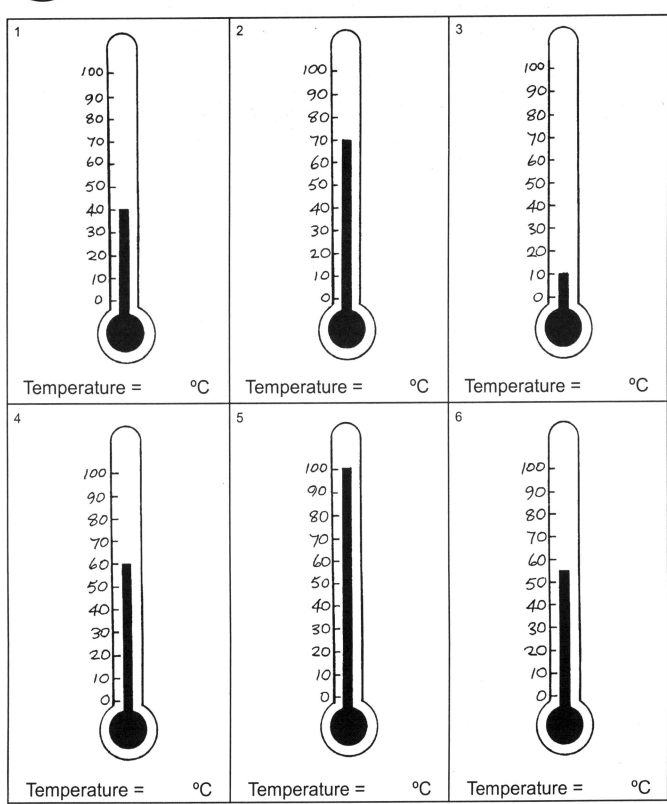

1

100
90
80
70
60
50
40
30
20
10
0

Temperature =   °C

2

100
90
80
70
60
50
40
30
20
10
0

Temperature =   °C

3

100
90
80
70
60
50
40
30
20
10
0

Temperature =   °C

4

100
90
80
70
60
50
40
30
20
10
0

Temperature =   °C

5

100
90
80
70
60
50
40
30
20
10
0

Temperature =   °C

6

100
90
80
70
60
50
40
30
20
10
0

Temperature =   °C

Measuring temperature

You need: a thermometer, a beaker of water,
tap water and a hot drink.

Activity Write what each of the objects is used to measure in the spaces below.
Use these words: time, temperature, weight and length.

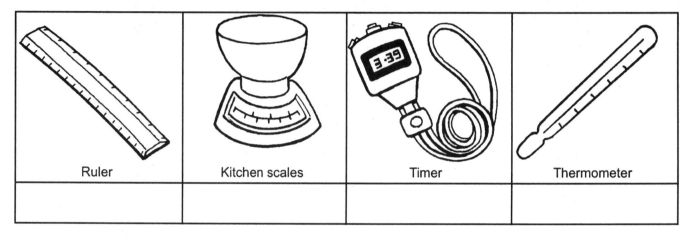

Ruler	Kitchen scales	Timer	Thermometer

We can measure how hot or cold water is by using a thermometer.

◆ Place the bulb of the
thermometer in a beaker of water.
The liquid inside the thermometer
will rise or fall and finally stay at a
steady level. The final level is the
temperature of the water.

The temperature of the water is _____ °C.

◆ Use a thermometer to carefully measure these temperatures.

	The cold water from the tap	**The air in your room**	**The air outside**	**Your teacher's tea**	**Your hand**
Temperature in degrees Celsius	°C	°C	°C	°C	°C

Reversible changes

You need: some salt, a spoon, a cup or beaker and a large flat plate.

Read A material's shape and form can be changed. Its **shape** can be changed by **squeezing** it. Its **form** can be changed by **heating** or **cooling** it.

Physical changes can normally be reversed. For example, water can be cooled to form ice and ice can be heated to form water.

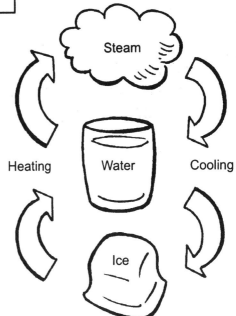

Steam

Heating   Water   Cooling

Ice

Activity Let's change some tap water by dissolving a spoonful of salt in it.

◆ Pour the salty water onto a large, clean plate and leave it in a warm place until all the water has evaporated.

◆ Examine the dry plate.

Answer Is dissolving a change that can be reversed?

Dissolving and stirring

You need: a measuring cylinder, sugar granules, a teaspoon and 2 beakers.

 Activity If you have ever wondered why people stir their tea after adding sugar then you should try this activity.

◆ Use a measuring cylinder to add 50 cm³ of tap water to two beakers.

◆ Carefully add a teaspoon of sugar to each of the beakers (add the sugar slowly to the water).

◆ Give **one** of the beakers a good stir with the teaspoon.

 Answer Look at both beakers. Can you suggest a reason why people stir their tea after adding sugar?

Dissolving and temperature

You need: a measuring cylinder, a thermometer, sugar granules, a teaspoon and 2 beakers.

 Let's investigate whether sugar dissolves faster in hot or cold water.

◆ Ask your teacher to add 50 cm³ of water from the hot tap to one beaker and 50 cm³ of water from the cold tap to the other beaker.

◆ Carefully measure the temperature of the water in each of the beakers.

Temperature of hot water	Temperature of cold water
°C	°C

◆ Slowly add a teaspoon of sugar to each of the beakers. Stir the water in each of the beakers five times.

Hot water

Cold water

◆ Record whether the sugar dissolves faster in the cold water or the hot water.

 Does the temperature of the water affect how quickly the sugar dissolves?

Dissolving and particle size

You need: a measuring cylinder, a teaspoon, sugar lumps, granulated sugar, caster sugar, 3 beakers and a timer.

 Activity Let's investigate whether the size of the particle affects the time it takes for a teaspoon of sugar to dissolve in water.

| Sugar lumps – large sugar particles | Granulated sugar – medium-size sugar particles | Caster sugar – small sugar particles |

◆ Add 50 cm³ of water to three beakers using a measuring cylinder.

◆ Add a teaspoonful of the three sugar samples to different beakers of water and stir.

◆ Time how long it takes for each type of sugar to dissolve.

Type of sugar	Time taken to dissolve
Sugar lumps	
Granulated sugar	
Caster sugar	

 Answer Does the size of the sugar particles affect how quickly the sugar dissolves?

Melting

You need: a glass, some ice and a thermometer.

Read

Ice will **melt** when it is placed in a glass of hot water because the water is hotter than the ice. Heat will flow from the water to the ice and melt it.

Activity

Let's investigate how quickly ice heats up when placed in a glass of cold tap water.

◆ Use a thermometer to measure the temperature of the water and room before you begin.

◆ Add four ice cubes to the glass of cold water. Measure the temperature every five minutes.

Temperature of the

water = _____ °C

Temperature of the

room = _____ °C

Time	Water temperature
At the start	°C
After 5 mins	°C
10 mins	°C
15 mins	°C
20 mins	°C
25 mins	°C
30 mins	°C
35 mins	°C
40 mins	°C
45 mins	°C
50 mins	°C
55 mins	°C
60 mins	°C
65 mins	°C
70 mins	°C
75 mins	°C
80 mins	°C
85 mins	°C
90 mins	°C
95 mins	°C
100 mins	°C
105 mins	°C
110 mins	°C
115 mins	°C
120 mins	°C
125 mins	°C

Melting and heat sources

 Read An ice cube will melt in your hand because your hand is hotter than the melting temperature of ice. Ice melts at 0 °C and your hand is around 32 °C. The heat from your hand flows to the ice, heating it up and causing it to melt.

 Activity Draw lines to match the objects below with one source of heat which could melt them.

Objects	**Sources of heat**

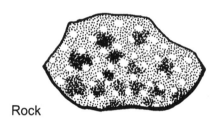

Rock

The Sun

Wax candle

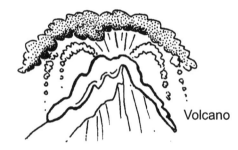

Volcano

Ice cream

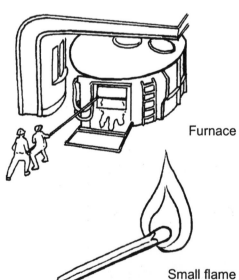

Furnace

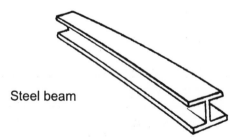

Steel beam

Small flame

Boiling

Read A clever scientist decides to boil some water for his tea on his small electric stove. Out of scientific interest he uses his IT sensor and computer to measure the temperature of the water every minute.

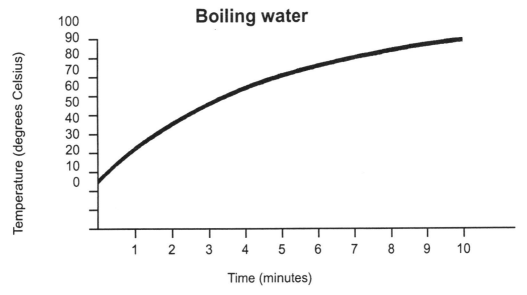

Boiling water

Temperature (degrees Celsius) vs Time (minutes)

Activity Study the graph from the IT sensor and predict at what temperature the water will boil.

Look further Ask your teacher to demonstrate in the classroom for you what the clever scientist did.

Condensing

You need: some ice and a glass with a lid.

 Read The air around us is made up of a mixture of gases (mostly nitrogen and oxygen) and **water vapour**.

The water vapour in the air cools into droplets of water to form clouds and eventually falls as rain.

When water vapour in the air cools down to form droplets of water we say it condenses.

 Activity This investigation will show if there is water vapour in the classroom.

◆ Put some ice and water into a glass and leave it for five minutes.

◆ The outside of the glass and the air around it will become cold.

Lid

 Answer Describe what you observe forming on the outside of the container.

Freezing

You need: a glass, ice, a thermometer and a fluffy towel.

Read **Freezing** is when a liquid, like water, changes to a solid, like ice. Every material has a temperature at which it freezes.

If ice is packed around water, the temperature of the water will drop. If the temperature drops far enough, the water will freeze.

Activity

◆ Try to find out at what temperature water will freeze by surrounding a small glass of water with ice.

◆ Wrap a towel around the ice to keep it close to the surface of the glass.

Temperature at the start	After 5 mins	After 10 mins	After 15 mins	After 20 mins	After 25 mins	After 30 mins
	°C	°C	°C	°C	°C	°C

Answer Use your results to try to predict at what temperature the water will freeze. It might help you to draw a graph.

Materials and their Properties

Evaporating

You need: some kitchen towel.

 Answer Look at these pictures. What do you think will happen to the water in the puddles?

Activity
◆ Wet your hands and then make a wet hand print on a paper towel.

◆ Watch what happens to your wet hand print.

 Answer What happens to your wet hand print after a while?

From liquid to gas

You need: some strong smelling perfume and a saucer.

Activity

◆ Work in a group for this investigation. One of you pours some perfume onto a saucer at the front of the classroom.

◆ As soon as one of the group smells the perfume, he or she should raise a hand.

◆ Use the space below to record what happens.

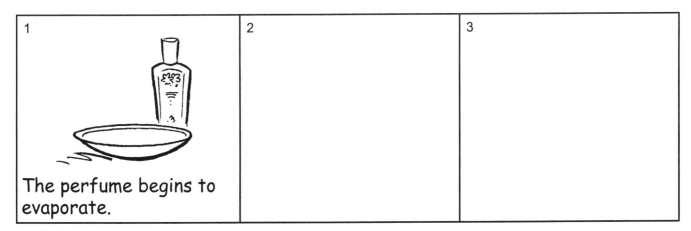

1	2	3
The perfume begins to evaporate.		

Answer

Can you explain what has happened? These words may help: nose, gas, evaporated and liquid.

The perfume is a _____ . Some of it has _____

and made a _____ , which has travelled to me. I can smell it

when it enters my _____ .

Look further

Find out why gas companies add a smell to natural gas for cookers and fires in our homes.

Materials and their Properties

Evaporation and air flow

You need: 2 pieces of filter paper, a water dropper, a timer and a hairdryer.

 Activity Let's find out whether flowing air helps water to evaporate more quickly.

◆ Using a dropper, put five drops of water onto two pieces of filter paper.

◆ Place one piece of filter paper on a desk away from draughts.

◆ Blow cool air over the other piece of filter paper with a hairdryer which is set to blow air only (not hot air).

◆ Time how long it takes for the water to evaporate.

Filter paper	Time taken for the water to evaporate
Left on the desk away from draughts	
Left on the desk with air blown over it	

 Answer Does flowing air affect how long it takes for water to evaporate?

The plate and bowl test

You need: a measuring cylinder, a dinner plate, a bowl and some food colouring.

 Activity Let's investigate whether water evaporates faster if the container has a large opening or a small opening at the top.

◆ Using a measuring cylinder, add 50 cm³ of water to three containers.

◆ Add some food colouring to the water so that it is easier to see.

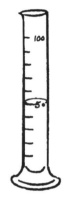

Dinner plate   Bowl   Measuring cylinder

◆ Leave the containers in a warm place and look at them each day.

 Answer Does the water evaporate faster from the plate, the bowl or the measuring cylinder?

Does the size of the container's opening affect how quickly the water evaporates?

The water cycle

You need: scissors, glue and some card and
the Resource sheet.

 Activity   Cut out and arrange the pictures and sentences into a story about
where rain comes from.

The raindrops fall down from the sky onto the Earth.	
The water vapour becomes cold as it rises into the sky where it **condenses** into small water droplets to form clouds.	
The clouds are blown over the hills where the small water droplets cool down to form raindrops.	
When the Sun shines on the water in the sea some water **evaporates** into **water vapour** and floats off up into the sky.	

 Activity   Cut out the words below and stick them in the correct positions on the
Resource sheet.

Evaporation	Sea	Heat from the Sun
Hill	Rain	Clouds
Condensation	Sky	River

The water cycle

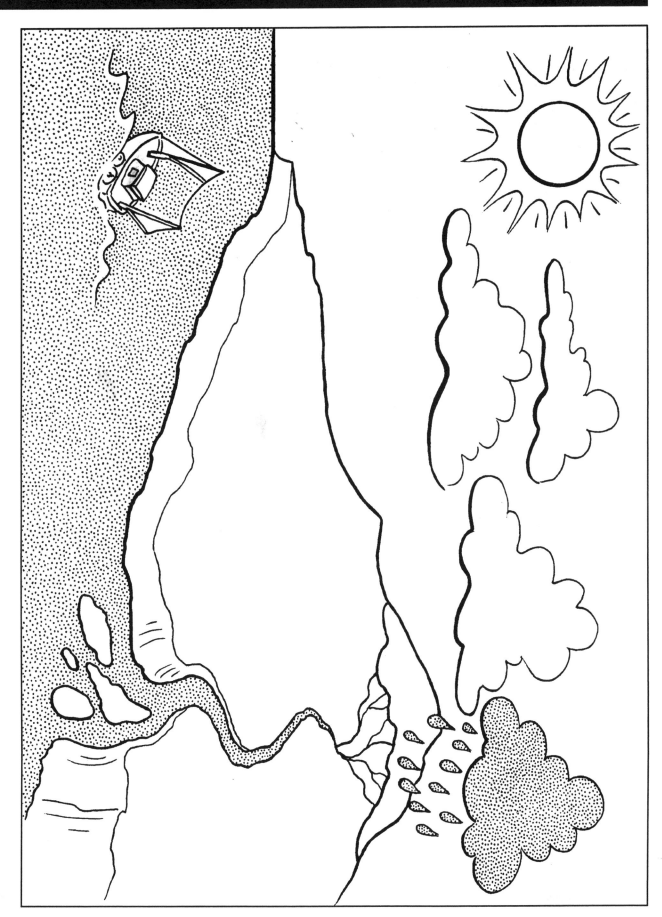

Non-reversible changes

Read Some changes in materials cannot be reversed. They are called **non-reversible changes**. The fire fighter called to a fire can only stop the non-reversible change from carrying on. The materials cannot be 'unburned' again.

Fire is a type of change called a **chemical change**. Chemical changes are very difficult or impossible to reverse.

Cooking is another example of a chemical change which is non-reversible. When an egg is boiled or fried it undergoes a chemical change which cannot be reversed. You cannot get the raw egg back again.

Activity Which of these changes are easily reversible and which are non-reversible? Put a tick by the non-reversible changes.

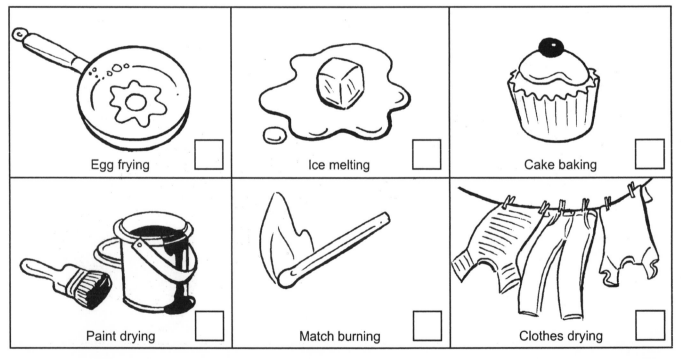

Egg frying ☐	Ice melting ☐	Cake baking ☐
Paint drying ☐	Match burning ☐	Clothes drying ☐

Rusting nails

You need: some transparent cups or beakers, some new, blunted nails, salt and grease.

 Read

When a nail is put in water there is a chemical change between the nail and the water called **rusting**. When something rusts it can become weak and may eventually break apart.

 Activity

◆ Place a clean, blunted iron nail in a beaker of clean water.

◆ Examine the nail each day and draw what you observe.

| Day 1 | Day 2 | Day 3 | Day 4 | Day 5 |

 Look further

You could investigate ways of preventing nails from rusting by setting up the following test.

  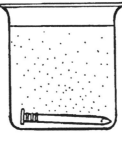 

Nail in air   Nail in water   Nail in salt water   Nail coated in grease and placed in water

Leave the nails for five days and then write down what you observe.

What changes?

You need: 6 beakers, Andrews salts, plaster of Paris, a lighter, vinegar, bicarbonate of soda, lemon juice and washing soda.

Read

We can often tell when a non-reversible change happens because we can actually see the change. Non-reversible changes happen when:
◆ we can see a gas being given off (bubbles);
◆ we can see a new substance is formed;
◆ we can see or feel light and heat being given off;
◆ we can see the colour change.

Activity

Watch your teacher as he/she demonstates the following non-reversible changes and write down why they are non-reversible.

| Andrews salts and water | Plaster of Paris and water | Petrol from a lighter |
| Vinegar and chalk | Gas from a cooker | Lemon juice and washing soda |

Protecting fire fighters

Read
When a non-reversible change takes place, like a fire, then heat and often poisonous gases are given off.

Activity
Use books and/or CD-ROMs to find out ways in which a fire fighter can be protected from the heat and poisonous fumes from a fire.

Look further

◆ Fire fighters have to know what the warning signs found on some dangerous materials mean.

◆ Find out what the signs mean and how fire fighters could protect themselves from these materials.

Materials and their Properties

Word search

Activity Use your knowledge and the clues below to find 10 words about materials changing.

1   This process cannot be reversed.
2   When water is boiled it changes into this gas.
3   When ice is placed in tap water it eventually disappears because it has

___ ___ ___ ___ ___ ___ .

4   A word used to describe water vapour in the air cooling to form droplets of water.
5   Water in a boiling pot will do this.
6   A change that can be reversed.
7   This kind of change, such as rusting, is impossible to reverse.
8   This helps water to evaporate more quickly (two words).
9   Water does this at 100 °C.
10 This instrument is used to measure temperature.

e	w	c	h	e	m	i	c	a	l	g	b
m	o	v	i	n	g	a	i	r	r	k	u
e	v	a	p	o	r	a	t	e	v	n	r
l	q	v	a	l	b	d	h	j	r	o	n
t	h	e	r	m	o	m	e	t	e	r	i
e	d	a	c	b	i	r	k	f	s	y	n
d	i	s	s	o	l	v	i	n	g	n	g
x	a	h	y	u	s	t	e	a	m	b	t
c	o	n	d	e	n	s	a	t	i	o	n

Separating Mixtures of Materials

Background information

A **mixture** is defined as something which is produced when two or more elements or compounds are joined together but are **not chemically bonded**. Mixtures can be solid–solid, liquid–liquid, gas–gas or any combination of each state. Mixtures can always be returned to their original constituents by a variety of chemical or physical means. Methods of separating mixtures include the following:

◆ A simple bar **magnet** can be used to separate a mixture where one of the constituents is magnetic (iron and sulphur powder mixture).

◆ Some solid–solid mixtures can be separated by **filtration** and **evaporation**. Water is added, the solution is filtered and then allowed to evaporate. This separation technique is only useful when one of the constituents is soluble in water (for example salt).

◆ Some liquid–solid mixtures can be separated by **distillation**. The best example of this process is the distillation of crude oil, which contains many dissolved solids and liquids. This technique makes use of the fact that different components of the oil have different boiling points: the oil is heated and the components tapped off as they boil and then condensed to be collected.

◆ A useful technique for separating liquid–liquid mixtures is **chromatography**. An example of this is in DNA testing, where

Helpful words	
Filtration	Electrolysis
Evaporation	Dissolve
Distillation	Saturated
Chromatography	Crystallization

scientists use the fact that proteins in the body move at different rates along the chromatography paper depending on their binding abilities.

◆ Electrical energy used to split solutions is called **electrolysis**. Components of the mixture can be collected at each electrode after an electrical current is passed through it.

A solid is added to a liquid (**solvent**) to produce a **solution**. The solid is also known as the **solute**. Some solids dissolve in water, or are **soluble**, others do not dissolve, or are **insoluble**. Salt can be dissolved in the water easily. If we could look at what the salt and water particles were doing, we would see that the salt particles were fitting into the spaces between the water particles.

Salt molecules

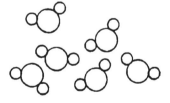

Water molecules

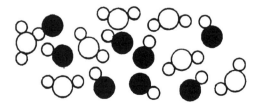

Salt and water mixture

Separating Mixtures of Materials

It is possible to keep adding salt until all the spaces between the water particles are full. When this point is reached the solution is **saturated**.

Crystals are formed when a solute is added to a warm saturated solution and then allowed to cool. The best example of this is copper sulphate, where copper crystals can be grown.

Some ideas for further work

◆ Use books and/or CD-ROMs to find out how gold prospectors in the past were able to separate gold from the soil using their pans.

◆ Find out how and why salt is separated from sea water in warm countries such as Spain.

◆ Use books and/or CD-ROMs to find out how sea water is turned into drinking water in desalination plants such as those in the Middle East.

◆ Find out about the ways in which an oil slick can be cleaned up from the sea and seashore.

◆ Investigate how mixtures are important in our lives. Think about hygiene (for example soap powders).

Separating Mixtures of Materials

Activity	Answers	Resources needed	Teaching/ safety notes
Sheet 1 (page 87) Sieving	The magnet is used to separate the paper clips from the sand, rice, peas and paper clips mixture. The large sieve is used to separate the peas, leaving the sand and rice. The flour sieve is then used to separate the rice leaving just the sand.	Scissors Glue Card	
Sheet 2 (page 88) Dissolving solids	• Soluble: powder paint, salt, cocoa, Andrews salts. • Insoluble: sand, flour, baking powder, plaster of Paris.	3 beakers Spoon Sugar Sand Flour Baking powder Powder paint Salt Plaster of Paris Cocoa Andrews salts	The plaster of Paris forms a white solid. The flour and baking powder settle on the bottom.
Sheet 3 (page 89) Filtering	• The sand and chalk do not dissolve in the water and are easily separated from the water by filtering. • The salt does dissolve in the water and cannot be separated from the water by filtering. • The particles of sand and chalk are much larger than the salt particles.	Sand Salt Chalk Measuring jug Basin Measuring cylinder Filter paper Magnifying glass	Filter paper has tiny holes in it. Water particles and salt particles pass through these holes but sand and chalk particles are too large to pass through the holes and become trapped by the filter paper.
Sheet 4 (page 90) Separating by evaporation	Powder paint, sugar and food colouring can be separated from the water by evaporation.	Powder paint Sugar Food colouring 3 saucers	Any solid material which dissolves in water can be separated from it again by evaporation. The water will have a lower boiling temperature than the solid and will therefore evaporate, leaving the solid behind.
Sheet 5 (page 91) Chromatography	As the water soaks up the filter paper and onto the ink spot, the spot dissolves. As the water continues upwards, it separates the colours which form the brown ink into yellow, green, purple and blue patches.	Filter paper Brown marker pen Beaker Stopwatch	It was found that water-based, washable and non-toxic pens worked well in this activity.

Separating Mixtures of Mateirals

Activity	Answers	Resources needed	Teaching/ safety notes
Sheet 6 (page 92) Sorting for recycling	These are the results for the selection of cans we used: **Can** **Is it magnetic?** beans yes coke no peas yes macaroni yes orange no	Strong magnet Tins Cans	
Sheet 7 (page 93) Different ways of separating	**Mixture** **Separated by** salty water evaporation dolly mixture hand steel & aluminium magnet powder paint evaporation gravel & sand sieving coloured bottles hand pile of clothes hand sand & water filtering		
Sheet 8 (page 94) Word search	1 magnet 2 evaporation 3 dissolves 4 insoluble 5 filtering 6 stir 7 water 8 sieve 9 temperature 10 flour		

Sieving

You need: scissors, glue and card.

Activity

Cut out and arrange the pictures below into a story telling how you could separate a mixture of sand, rice, peas and paper clips.

Here is a mixture of sand, rice, peas and paper clips to begin your story.

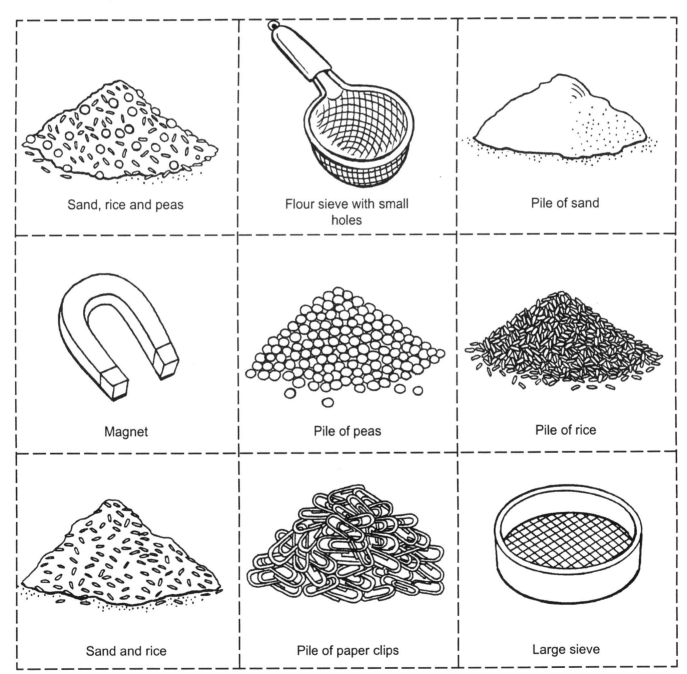

Sand, rice and peas	Flour sieve with small holes	Pile of sand
Magnet	Pile of peas	Pile of rice
Sand and rice	Pile of paper clips	Large sieve

Materials and their Properties

Dissolving solids

You need: 3 beakers, a spoon, sugar, sand, flour, baking powder, powder paint, salt, plaster of Paris, cocoa and Andrews salts.

 Read If you put sugar in tea and stir it, the sugar seems to disappear. This is because the sugar has **dissolved** in the water.

If you put sand in water and stir it, the sand just sinks to the bottom. This is because the sand does not dissolve – it is **insoluble**.

Some substances, like flour, colour the water. This is called a **suspension**. If you leave it to settle for a day, the flour will sink to the bottom.

 Activity Add some sugar, sand and flour to different beakers of water and stir them.

Sugar dissolves in water   Sand is insoluble   Flour forms a suspension

Put a tick in the column to show whether these substances are soluble or insoluble in water.

Substance	Soluble?	Insoluble?
Sand		
Flour		
Baking powder		
Powder paint		
Salt		
Plaster of Paris		
Cocoa		
Andrews salts		

Filtering

You need: sand, salt, chalk, a measuring jug, a basin, a measuring cylinder, filter paper and a magnifying glass.

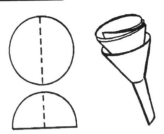

◆ Mix some sand into a measuring jug containing water.

◆ Put a filter paper into a funnel as shown.

◆ Try to separate the sand from the water by pouring it through the filter paper.

◆ Repeat this activity with a salt and water mixture and a chalk and water mixture.

Are you able to separate the sand or chalk from the water by filtering?

What about the salt? Can you separate it from the water by filtering?

Are the sand and chalk soluble or insoluble?

Examine some dry sand, chalk and salt with a magnifying glass. What do you observe about the size of the sand, chalk and salt particles?

Separating by evaporation

You need: powder paint, sugar, food colouring and 3 saucers.

 Read Salt can be separated from salty water by allowing the water to evaporate. The solid salt is left behind.

 Activity Let's find out whether this method works with solutions of powder paint, sugar and food colouring.

Put some of the solutions in separate saucers and then place them in a warm place.

What happens?

Chromatography

You need: filter paper, brown marker pen, a beaker and a stopwatch.

 Activity   Some mixtures can be separated by chromatography.

◆ Cut out a strip of filter paper about 1 cm wide and 10 cm long.

◆ Make a large ink spot near the bottom of the paper with a brown marker.

◆ Put a little water in a beaker.

◆ Hang the filter paper over the edge of the beaker so that the edge near the dot is touching the water.

◆ Leave it for 10 minutes.

Make sure the edge of the paper nearest the ink spot just touches the water.

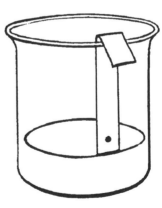

 Answer   What happens to the ink spot?

Sorting for recycling

You need: a strong magnet and a selection of tins and cans.

 Read It is important to recycle things like bottles, paper and cans so that they can be used again.

People often sort coloured glass bottles by putting them into separate bottle banks.

 Activity Where is the nearest bottle bank to your school or home?

 Read In recycling plants tin cans made of steel are separated from aluminium cans by using very strong magnets.

 Activity Use a magnet to find out which tins and cans are steel and which are aluminium.

Can	Is it magnetic? (made of steel)

Different ways of separating

 Activity Match the mixtures below with a method of separating them. The first one is done for you.

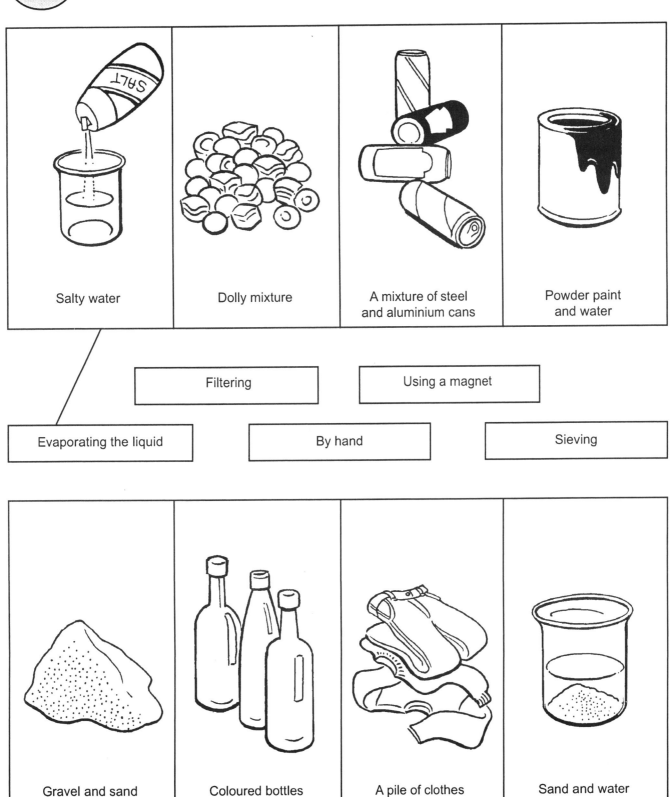

| Salty water | Dolly mixture | A mixture of steel and aluminium cans | Powder paint and water |

Filtering

Using a magnet

Evaporating the liquid

By hand

Sieving

| Gravel and sand | Coloured bottles | A pile of clothes | Sand and water |

Materials and their Properties

Word search

Use your knowledge and the clues below to find ten words about mixtures and ways in which they can be separated.

1   This object can be used to separate a mixture of iron and chalk.
2   This technique can be used to separate a mixture of salt and water.
3   Salt seems to disappear in water because it __ __ __ __ __ __ __ __ __ .
4   Sand lies at the bottom of water and doesn't dissolve because it is

   __ __ __ __ __ __ __ __ __ .
5   This technique can be used to separate sand from water.
6   You do this to help sugar dissolve in tea.
7   This liquid is good at dissolving dirt from your hands.
8   Stones in soil can be recovered using this kitchen utensil.
9   Water can dissolve more solid (like salt) by increasing its

   __ __ __ __ __ __ __ __ __ __ __ .
10 When added to water this substance forms a suspension.

y	s	d	i	s	s	o	l	v	e	s
f	i	l	t	e	r	i	n	g	v	b
t	e	m	p	e	r	a	t	u	r	e
e	v	a	p	o	r	a	t	i	o	n
c	e	g	e	h	n	f	d	e	s	f
t	u	n	i	o	f	l	o	u	r	p
q	s	e	e	w	a	t	e	r	o	f
a	s	t	i	r	z	x	d	j	i	l
t	r	i	n	s	o	l	u	b	l	e

Glossary

These definitions, while accurate, are by no means comprehensive. If you require a more exact definition, you should consult a good scientific dictionary.

atom
The smallest building block of matter; all matter is made up of a number of atoms.

chromatography
A method of separating solutes by using porous materials like paper.

condensation
What happens when a gas cools to form a liquid. An everyday example is steam from a kettle of boiling water cooling and running down a window.

crystallization
A method of forming crystals by adding a solute to an already saturated solution, then allowing it to cool (a solution is a mixture of a solute or solutes and a liquid solvent).

dissolve
To make a solid or a gas apparently 'disappear' by mixing it with a liquid.

distillation
A method of separating different liquids by using their different boiling points. As the mixture is boiled, the different liquids become gases at different temperatures. These gases are collected and, as they cool, they return to liquid form.

electrolysis
A method of separating a solution into its constituent parts by passing electricity through it.

element
An element is made up of only one type of atom; gold, oxygen and iron are elements.

evaporation
The changing of a liquid from a gas by heating it or leaving it exposed to air. For example, water evaporates as it is heated but puddles also evaporate after a time.

filtering and evaporating
The means by which a solution of a soluble solid, an insoluble solid and a liquid can be separated. The last part of the process involves evaporation.

freezing
When a liquid cools to such an extent that it becomes a solid. Different liquids freeze at different temperatures.

igneous
A type of rock which pushes its way, in a liquid form, from beneath the Earth's crust. On the surface it cools and solidifies. It can be seen forming in the action of volcanoes.

man-made
Any material which is not found naturally, but which uses natural materials in its construction.

melting
The process by which a solid changes to a liquid when heated.

metamorphic
A type of rock which has been changed from its original state by being squeezed or being heated to a great temperature.

particles
A group of atoms.

Periodic Table
Everything in and around Earth is either a chemical element or an amalgamation of two or more chemical elements (compounds). These elements are arranged according to their chemical and physical properties into what is known as the Periodic Table. There are around 100 known elements in the Periodic Table.

reversible/non-reversible changes
Materials can be changed, for example by changes in temperature or by being squeezed. Some changes are not permanent but some are. If you squeeze a tennis ball, its change of shape is reversible. If you burn coal in a fire, then this is most certainly irreversible.

saturated
If you mix a soluble material in a liquid, the material will dissolve. However, there is a limit to how much of the material the liquid will dissolve. When it reaches this limit, and the material no longer dissolves, the liquid is saturated.

sedimentary
A type of rock which has been eroded, sunk beneath water and then compressed to form another type of rock.

solute
Any solid which has been dissolved in a liquid.